NATIONAL GEOGRAPHIC

Blood

CELLS AT WORK

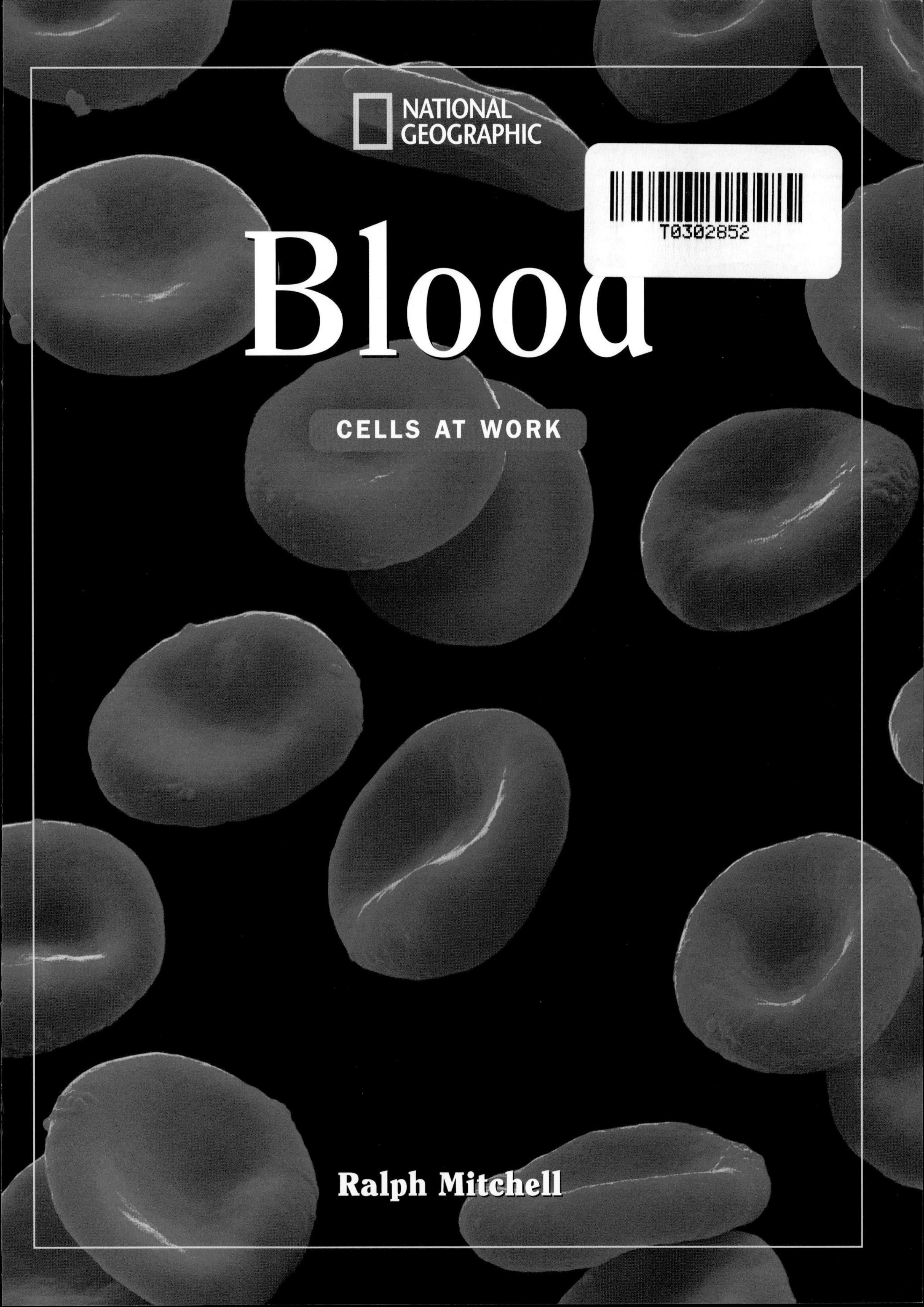

Ralph Mitchell

PICTURE CREDITS

Cover: photograph of a girl examining a cut on her arm (center left) © Stock Image Group/SPL; illustration of circulatory system (bottom left) by Dave Gunson; scanning electron micrograph (SEM) of human red blood cells (right) © Stone/Getty Images.

Photographs: page 1 © Andrew Syred/Stone/Getty Images; page 4 (bottom left) © Jim Zuckerman/Corbis/Tranz; page 4 (bottom right) Photodisc; page 5 (top) © Stock Image Group/SPL; page 5 (bottom left) Corbis/Tranz; page 5 (bottom right) © Lester V. Bergman/Corbis/Tranz; page 9 © Stock Image Group/SPL; page 10 © Andrew Syred/Stone/Getty Images; page 11 (top) © Stock Image Group/SPL; page 11 (bottom) © Stock Image Group/SPL; page 12 © VO Trung Dung/Corbis/Tranz; page 13 © Stock Image Group/SPL; page 14 © Stock Image Group/SPL; page 19 © Michael Keller/Corbis/Tranz; page 20 © Mark L. Stephenson/Corbis/Tranz; page 21 Photodisc; page 22 © Stock Image Group/SPL; page 23 (bottom left) © Astier Frederik/Corbis/Tranz; page 23 (bottom right) © Cheryl Diaz Meyer/Dallas Morning News/Corbis/Tranz; page 24 © David C. Tomlinson/Stone/Getty Images; page 25 © Lester V. Bergman/Corbis/Tranz; page 26 (bottom left) © Leif Skoogfors/Corbis/Tranz; page 26 (bottom right) © Ted Spiegel/Corbis/Tranz; page 29 © Mary Kate Denny/Stone/Getty Images.

Illustrations on pages 7, 8, and 17 by Dave Gunson.

Produced through the worldwide resources of the National Geographic Society, John M. Fahey, Jr., President and Chief Executive Officer; Gilbert M. Grosvenor, Chairman of the Board; Nina D. Hoffman, Executive Vice President and President, Books and Education Publishing Group.

PREPARED BY NATIONAL GEOGRAPHIC SCHOOL PUBLISHING
Ericka Markman, Senior Vice President and President, Children's Books and Education Publishing Group; Steve Mico, Vice President and Editorial Director; Marianne Hiland, Executive Editor; Richard Easby, Editorial Manager; Jim Hiscott, Design Manager; Kristin Hanneman, Illustrations Manager; Matt Wascavage, Manager of Publishing Services; Sean Philpotts, Production Manager.

EDITORIAL MANAGEMENT
Morrison BookWorks, LLC

PROGRAM CONSULTANTS
Dr. Shirley V. Dickson, Program Director, Literacy, Education Commission of the States; James A. Shymansky, E. Desmond Lee Professor of Science Education, University of Missouri-St. Louis.

National Geographic Theme Sets program developed by Macmillan Education Australia, Pty Limited.

Published by the National Geographic Society
1145 17th Street, N.W.
Washington, D.C. 20036-4688

ISBN: 978-0-7922-4732-6
ISBN: 0-7922-4732-9

Product 41972

Printed in China

14 15 16 17 18 19 20 21
10 9 8 7 6

Contents

Cells at Work

Did you know that every living creature on Earth is made up of cells? Most cells are so tiny you can't see them, even with a magnifying glass. You need to use a powerful tool called a microscope to see cells. Different types of cells—like skin cells, muscle cells, blood cells, and bone cells—do different jobs.

Key Concepts

1. **All organisms are made up of cells that carry out processes that are needed to live.**
2. **Specialized cells perform specialized functions in organisms.**
3. **Sometimes cells get a disease or become damaged and don't function as they should.**

Four Kinds of Cells

Skin

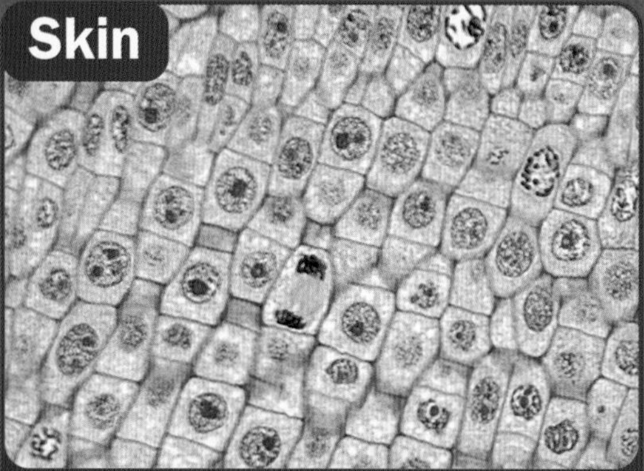

The cells on the surface of your skin are loose and flaky.

Muscle

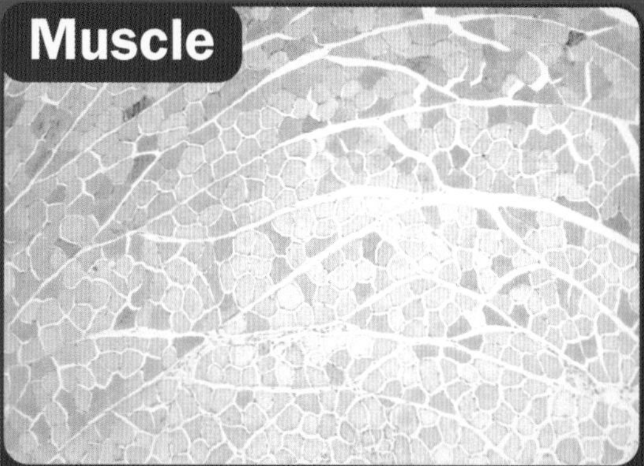

The cells of your muscles are packed together.

In this book you will learn about the cells that make up your blood.

Blood

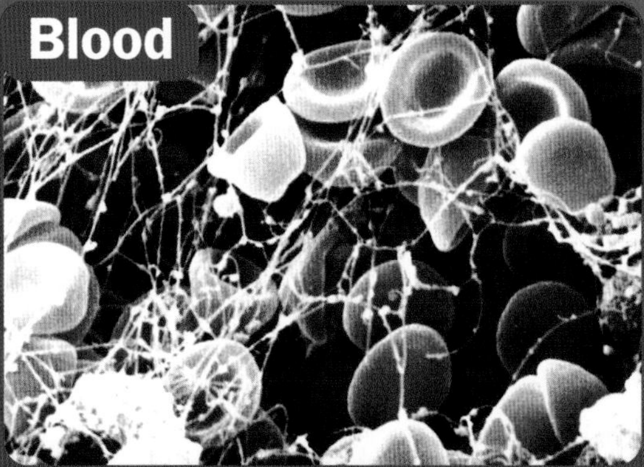

The cells in your blood float in a liquid.

Bone

Some bone cells are arranged in tight circles.

Cells and Your Blood

Have you ever cut yourself badly enough for blood to flow? What color was the blood? Do you know what would have happened if germs had gotten into the cut? You can learn some things about blood just by looking at it. To really understand blood, however, you need to know what blood cells do.

Key Concept 1 **All organisms are made up of cells that carry out processes that are needed to live.**

Organisms and Cells

Organisms are living things with one or more parts that work to keep them alive. There are many kinds of organisms, such as plants, people, and other animals. **Cells** are the smallest living parts of all organisms. Some organisms have only one cell. But most organisms, from ants to alligators, are made up of many cells. There are more than 200 different types of cells in the human body.

organisms
all living things, including animals, plants, and single-celled life-forms

cells
the smallest living parts of organisms

Because cells are parts of organisms, they do all of the things that organisms do. Cells grow and make new cells. Cells respond to their environment, or the things around them. They also use energy and get rid of waste. Different cells have different functions. The size and shape of a cell depends on its function.

All cells have three main parts—a **cell membrane**, a **nucleus**, and **cytoplasm**. The cell membrane surrounds the cell. Inside the cell is the nucleus, one of the largest parts of the cell, which controls what the cell does. The rest of the cell is filled by a jelly-like substance called cytoplasm. Cytoplasm contains chemicals that help the cell work.

Look at the diagram. It shows the three main parts of a cell.

Parts of a Cell

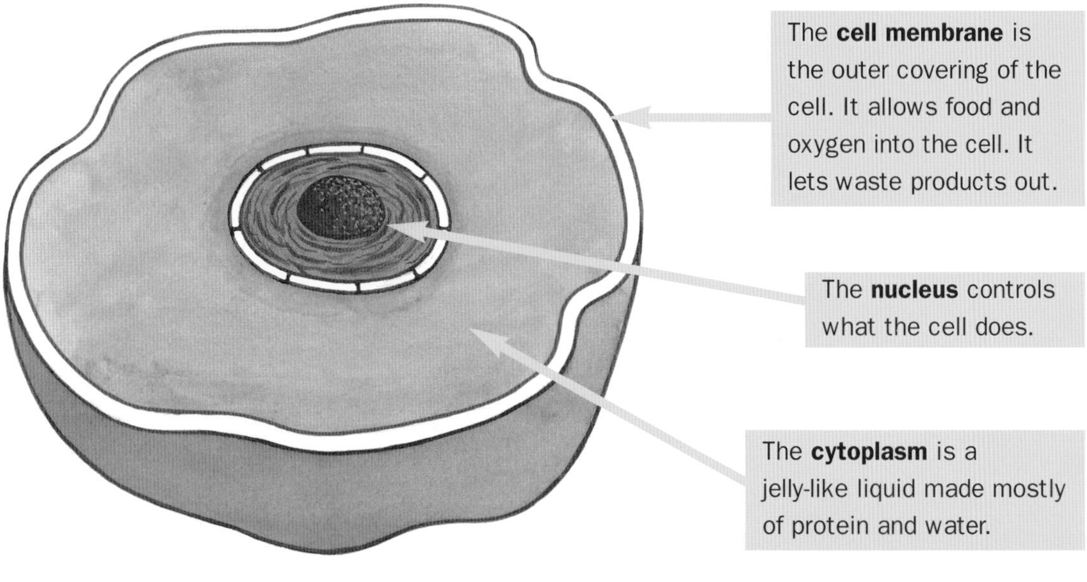

Blood and Blood Cells

The cells that make up blood are **specialized** cells. This means that they perform a particular task or function. Red blood cells, white blood cells, **platelets**, and a liquid called **plasma** are all parts of blood. They work together to keep the body functioning.

specialized
able to perform one special task or function

Blood is circulated, or moved, around your body by your heart, which is a large muscle. The heart pushes blood through a system of tubes called blood vessels. Large blood vessels are called arteries and veins. The heart and the blood vessels join together to form the circulatory system.

Circulatory System

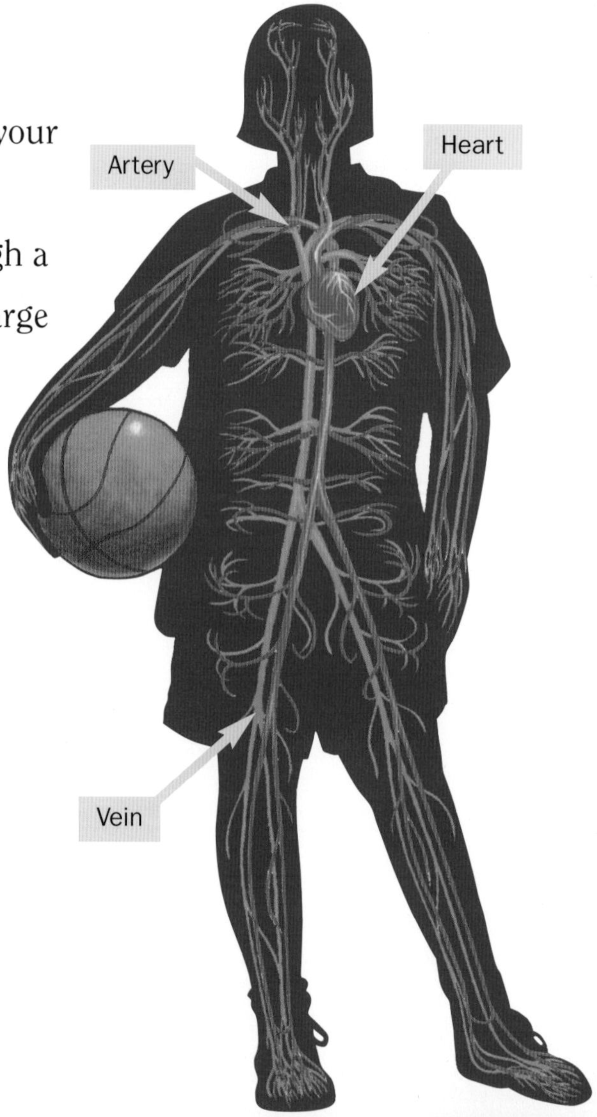

The circulatory system circulates, or moves, blood around your body. Without fresh blood, cells would die. Blood transports **nutrients** and oxygen to cells and carries away wastes. One of these wastes is carbon dioxide. Carbon dioxide is produced when your cells use oxygen for energy.

Your body has to make about 150 million blood cells every minute of your life to replace the ones that die. Red blood cells live about 120 days. White blood cells can live for much longer. Platelets only circulate in the blood for about four days before they die. Dead platelets are removed by white blood cells.

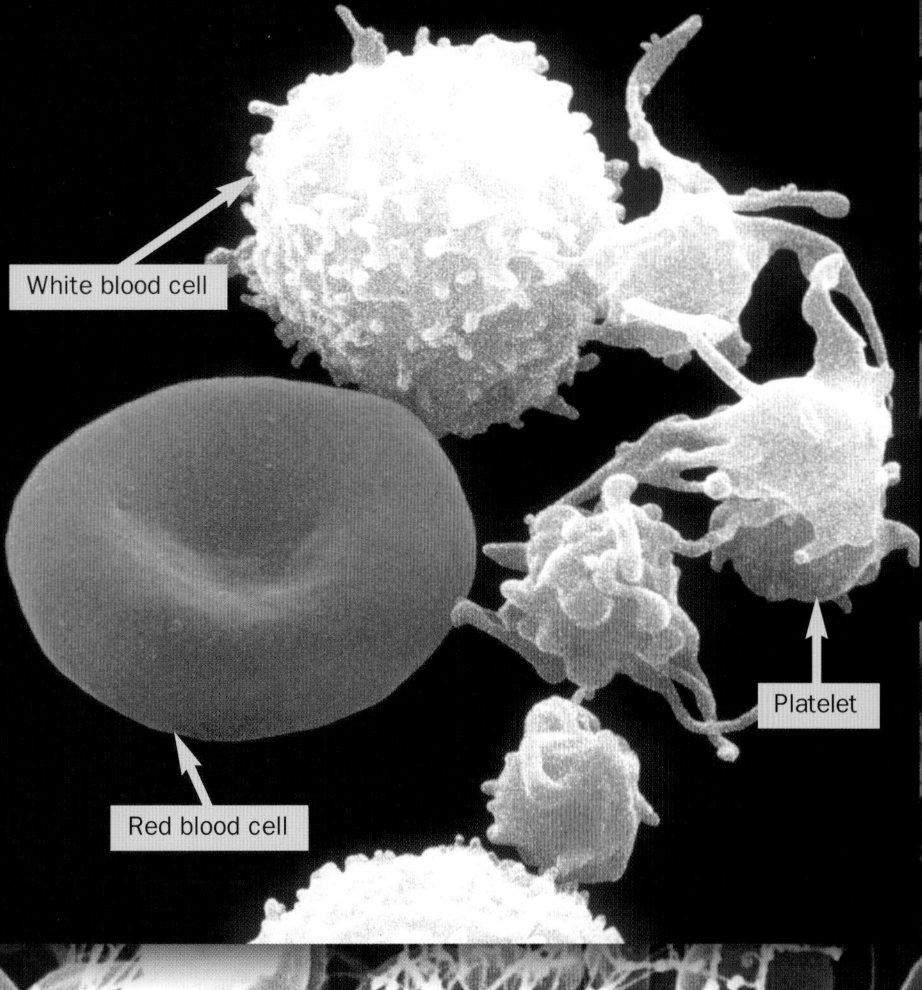

What Do Blood Cells Do?

Because each type of blood cell is specialized, each type performs different functions. White blood cells cannot do the work of red blood cells. Platelets cannot do the work of white blood cells.

Red Blood Cells Red blood cells carry oxygen around the body to all of the other cells. Red blood cells contain a substance called **hemoglobin** that picks up oxygen when a person breathes. The oxygen is then carried around the body by red blood cells to other body cells, which all need oxygen to live. A tiny drop of blood contains about five million red blood cells. Red blood cells are made in the **bone marrow**.

White Blood Cells White blood cells also have a specialized job to do. Like red blood cells, they are made in the bone marrow. They are larger than red blood cells and there are fewer of them. There is about one white cell for every 700 red cells. The specialized job of white blood cells is to defend the body against infection caused by things like germs, viruses, and bacteria.

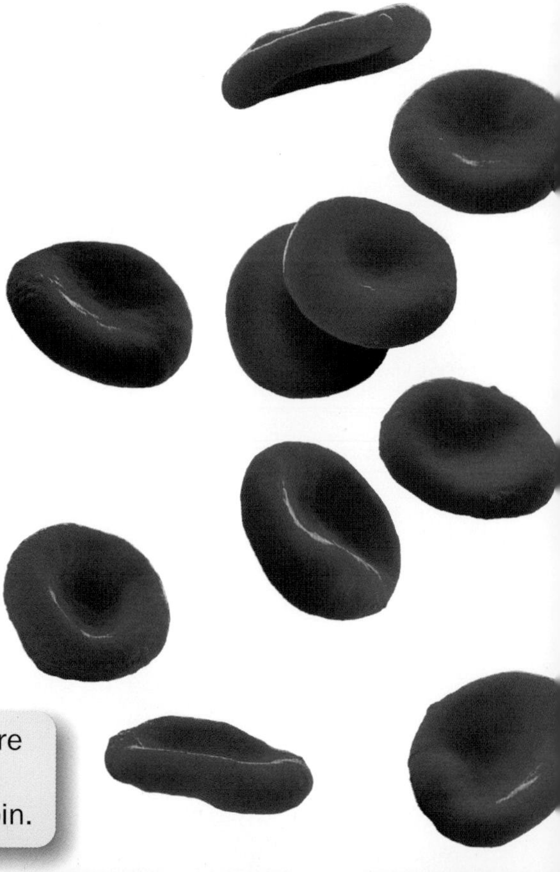

Red blood cells are red because they contain hemoglobin.

If harmful bacteria or viruses enter the body, white blood cells are activated. They travel to the infected area and kill the bacteria or viruses. To fight serious infections, the body produces more white cells. White blood cells can even destroy cells that cause cancer.

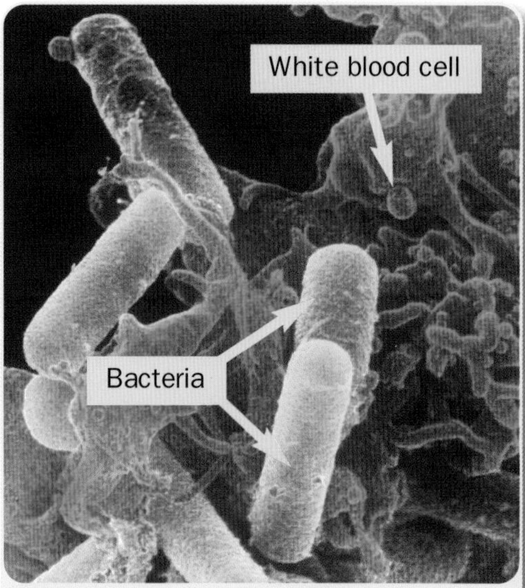

This white blood cell is swallowing up bacteria cells.

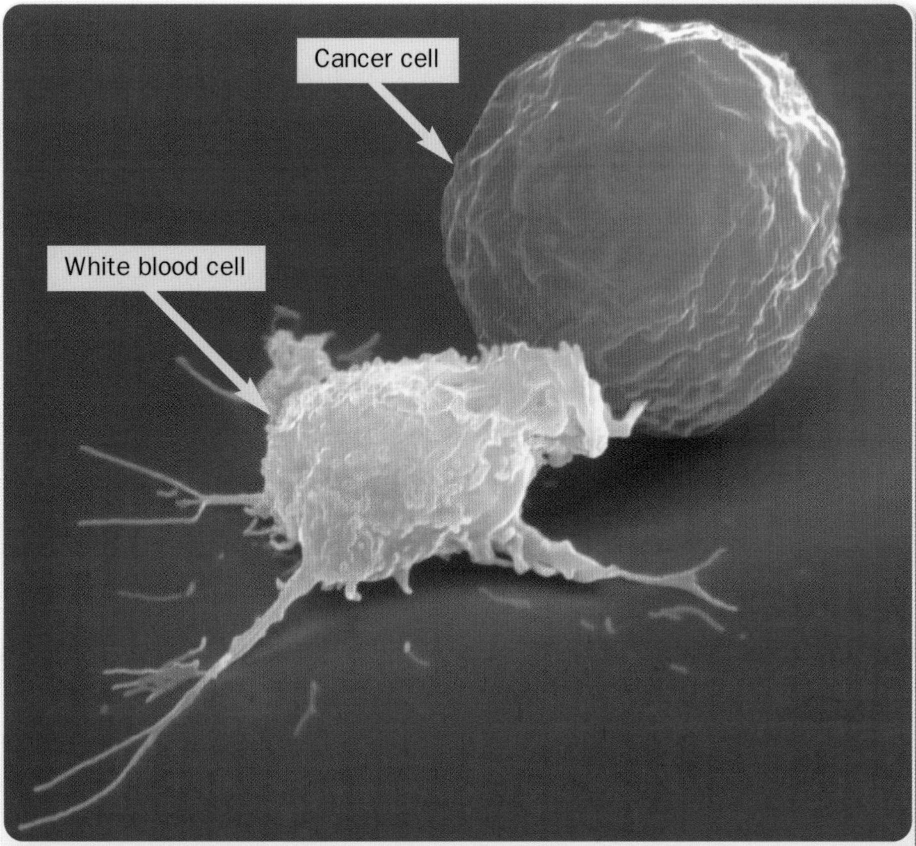

This cancer cell is being attacked by a white blood cell.

Platelets Platelets are tiny cell-like disks. They make chemicals that help blood **clot**. Clotting makes blood thicken and dry once it comes into contact with air. If blood did not clot, wounds would not stop bleeding.

If the body is bleeding from a cut or wound, platelets stick together to form a clot. The blood clot dries and shrinks, pulling the edges of the wound together to make a scab. If viruses or bacteria get into the cut, white blood cells fight them. White blood cells also clean away any dead cells and clotted blood.

Plasma Plasma is the liquid part of your blood that contains no blood cells. It is straw-colored and is about 90 percent water. Plasma makes up about 50 to 60 percent of your blood. Red and white blood cells and platelets make up the rest. Plasma carries nutrients from digested food. It also carries away waste products from cells.

Plasma is what is left when all of the blood cells have been removed from blood.

Key Concept 3 Sometimes cells get a disease or become damaged and don't function as they should.

Blood and Disease

When blood cells are damaged or have a **disease**, they do not work as they should. For example, damaged white blood cells prevent the body from fighting off many serious illnesses.

disease
a condition that keeps an organism from working as it should

Sickle Cell Anemia One disease of the blood is sickle cell anemia. It causes changes in the **structure** of blood cells. A cell's structure is its size and shape, and the way it fits together with other cells. People with sickle cell anemia have an abnormal type of hemoglobin that causes red blood cells to change their shape from round to sickle-shaped. Because sickle-shaped cells do not flow easily through small blood vessels, they can become trapped and cause blockages, which result in pain and fever. In serious cases the blockages can cause lung or kidney damage, or even death.

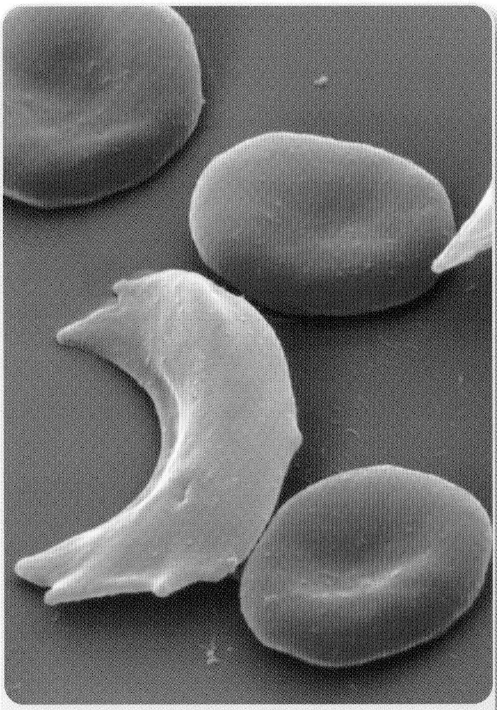
A sickle-shaped red blood cell

Sickle cell anemia can sometimes be cured by a bone marrow transplant. This means replacing cells in the bone marrow with cells from a healthy person.

Human Immunodeficiency Virus (HIV) Another disease that alters the structure of blood cells is HIV. This virus infects white blood cells. It enters some types of white blood cells and then reproduces itself. The virus stops the white blood cells from functioning the way they should. As the virus reproduces, it infects more and more white blood cells. The infected cells begin to die and the body loses its ability to fight infections.

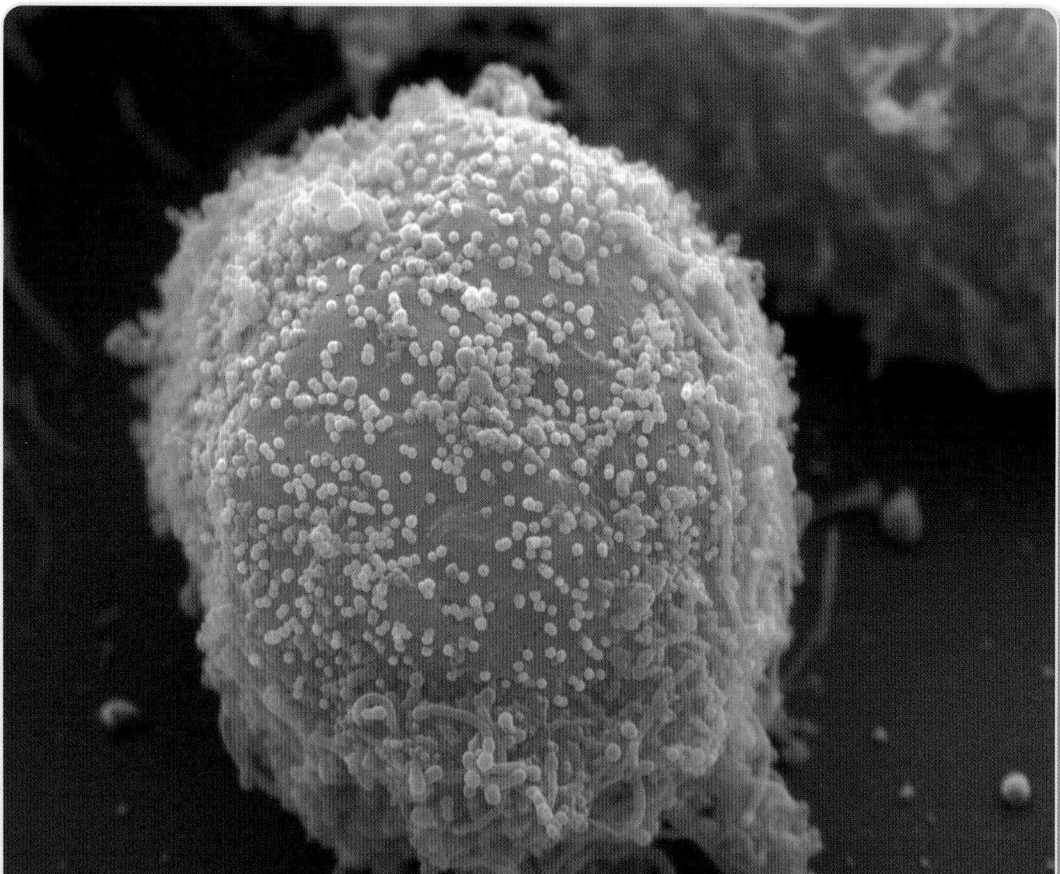

Blue particles of HIV are attached to the surface of this white blood cell. Here the white blood cell is shown as yellow.

Think About the Key Concepts

Think about what you read. Think about the pictures and diagrams. Use these to answer the questions. Share what you think with others.

1. Why are cells important to living organisms?

2. What are some of the things that all cells do?

3. Name some specialized cells and describe the different kinds of work they do.

4. What are some injuries or diseases that can be caused by damaged cells?

VISUAL LITERACY

Labeled Diagram

Diagrams are pictures that show information.
You can learn new ideas without having to read many words. Diagrams use pictures and words to explain ideas.

There are different kinds of diagrams.
This diagram of a blood vessel is a **labeled diagram**. A labeled diagram is a picture that shows the parts of something. It helps show how something works. Look back at the diagram on page 7. It is a labeled diagram of the parts of a cell.

How to Read a Diagram

1. **Read the title.**
   The title tells you what the diagram is about.
2. **Read the labels and captions.**
   Labels name the parts of the diagram. Captions give information about the parts.
3. **Study the diagram.**
   Use the labels and captions to help you understand the diagram.
4. **Think about what you learned.**
   Decide what new information you learned from the diagram.

Inside a Blood Vessel

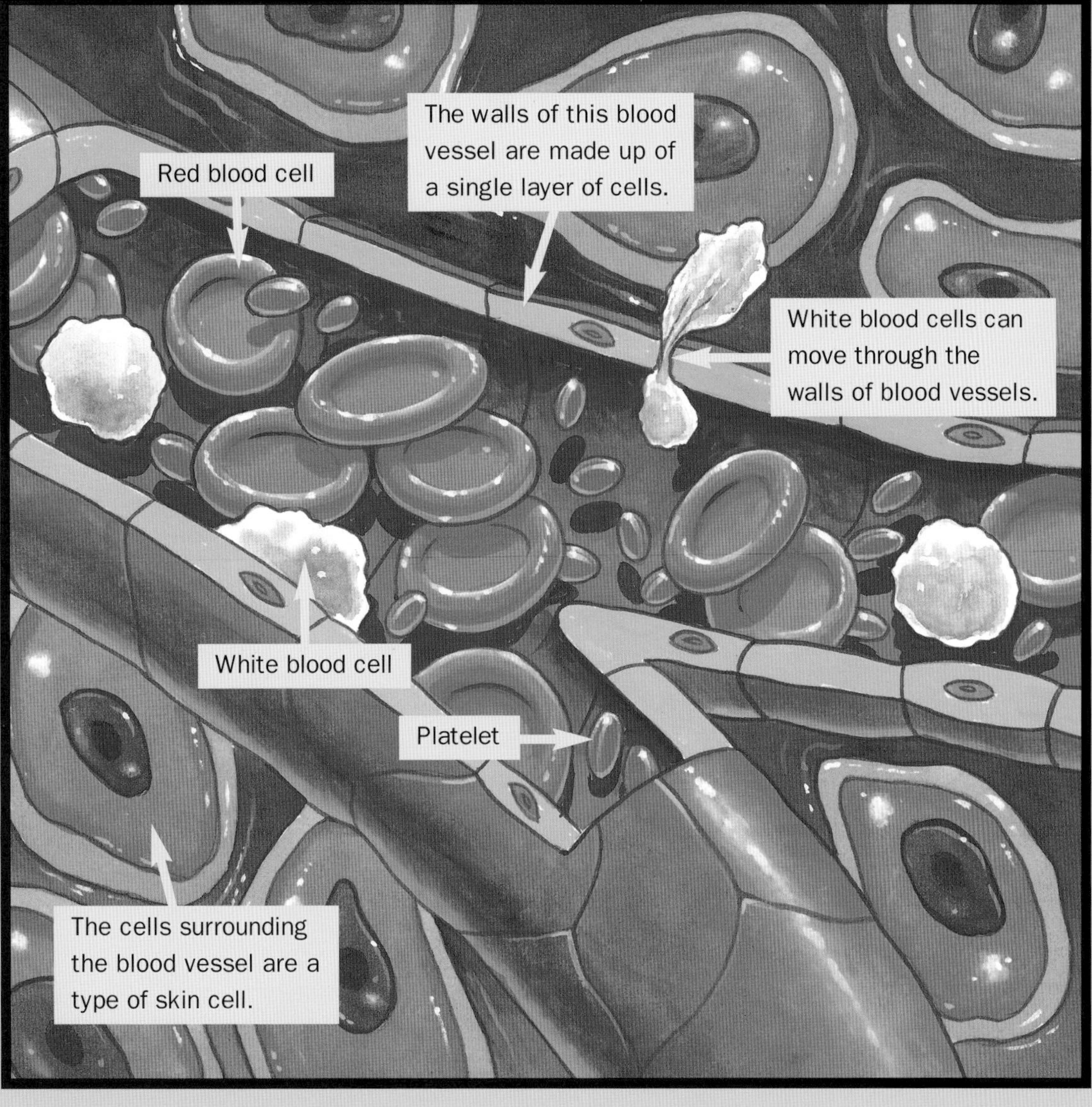

What's Inside?

Read the diagram by following the steps on page 16. Write down all the things you found out about what's inside a blood vessel. Explain what you learned to a classmate. See if your classmate understood the diagram the same way you did.

GENRE STUDY

Informational Pamphlet

An **informational pamphlet** gives brief but important information about a topic. The pamphlet starting on page 19 gives health information about you and your blood.

An informational pamphlet includes the following:

Headings
The headings are large and easy to read. They allow the reader to see quickly what a section is about. Headings are often questions.

Text Paragraphs
The text paragraphs give detailed information. They answer the questions in the headings.

Checklists and Other Lists
Lists present shortened forms of important information that are easy to remember.

You and Your Blood

The **title** introduces the topic.

How do I keep my blood healthy?

Headings often contain questions that tell you what you are going to read about.

There are things you can do to keep your blood healthy. You can eat foods with enough iron to protect yourself against blood diseases such as iron-deficiency anemia. Through immunization, you can also help your blood to protect you from disease. And finally, you can watch for any signs of the most serious blood disease—leukemia.

Text paragraphs answer the questions in the headings.

Photographs add interest to the topic.

Lists summarize basic facts.

Healthy Blood Checklist

- ☐ Eat iron-rich foods.
- ☐ Get immunized.
- ☐ Check for signs of blood disease.

Healthy blood needs a healthy diet.

What is iron-deficiency anemia?

Iron-deficiency anemia is a disease caused by having too little iron in your body. To stay healthy, your blood cells need an adequate supply of iron. Iron is a mineral that is found naturally in certain foods. You get iron from such foods as red meat, poultry, spinach, and dried apricots. If you do not get enough iron, you may be at risk of an iron deficiency, which is a lack of iron.

Red blood cells

Iron makes up an important part of your hemoglobin. Hemoglobin is in the red blood cells. It carries oxygen from your lungs to all the cells throughout the body. If the cells in your body do not get enough oxygen, you can begin to feel weak and tired. Over a long period of time you can develop iron-deficiency anemia.

What causes iron-deficiency anemia?

Iron-deficiency anemia is a disease caused by a lack of iron in your blood. It can be caused by a lack of iron in your diet. It can also happen when your body is changing. For example, if you are a teenager you use more iron because your body is growing so quickly. If you are injured and lose a lot of blood, that can also lead to a lack of iron.

What are the symptoms of iron-deficiency anemia?

Iron-deficiency anemia can make you feel weak and tired. You might have trouble concentrating and find it harder to learn. You may also feel cold. Sometimes your body is less able to fight infections.

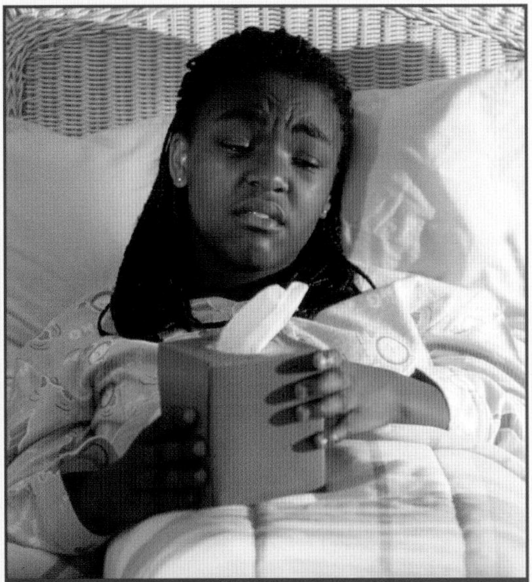

Iron-deficiency anemia can lead to other illnesses.

Luckily, it is usually easy to treat iron-deficiency anemia. Make sure you have enough iron in your diet and you can soon be your energetic self again.

Iron-rich foods

- **Meat**
  liver, beef, turkey, chicken
- **Fish**
  cod, oysters, clams, sardines
- **Vegetables**
  spinach, potatoes (with skin), dried kidney beans, lentils, soybeans, tofu
- **Fruit**
  dried apricots, raisins, prunes
- **Cereals**
  branflakes, wheatgerm, enriched cereals
- **Other**
  molasses, seaweed, cashew nuts, pumpkin seeds

What is immunization?

To be healthy, your body needs to avoid disease. Immunization is a method of giving immunity, or protection, from certain diseases. It gives your blood ways to fight disease. Immunization has been very important in controlling some diseases, such as tuberculosis and polio.

How does it work?

Immunization, or vaccination, works in two ways. The first way uses mild forms of actual diseases. These are injected into the body and make your white blood cells produce the right type of antibodies. Antibodies are substances that the body makes to detect viruses or bacteria. The process takes a little time. But in about two weeks you should have immunity.

If you catch one of the diseases you have been immunized for, your antibodies will recognize it. They will signal the white blood cells to destroy it right away.

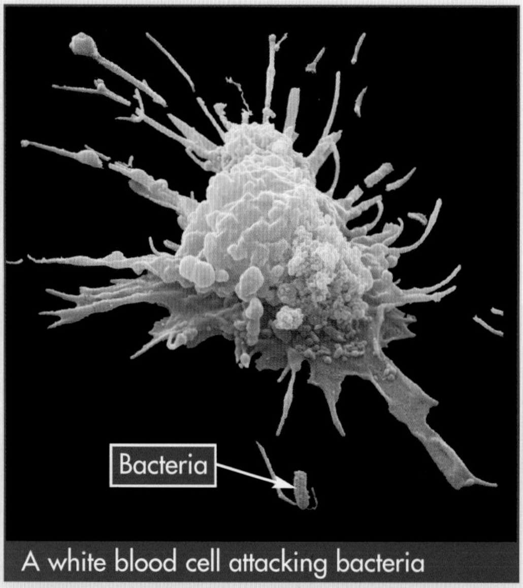

A white blood cell attacking bacteria

The second way of immunizing uses antibodies that have not been made by your body. The antibodies have been made in a laboratory instead. They are then injected into your body. Antibodies target the virus or bacteria cells and stop them from spreading. They will start to protect a person from infection right away.

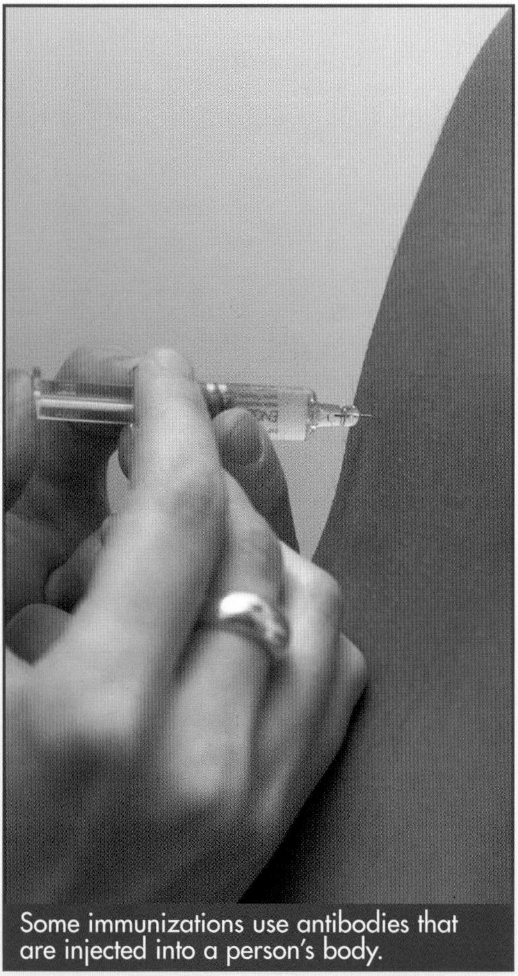

Some immunizations use antibodies that are injected into a person's body.

Do immunizations cause side effects?

Immunization injections can sometimes have side effects. Usually they are mild, such as soreness or redness at the injection site. Sometimes they are more serious, like fever and pain in the joints. Reactions may sometimes be severe but this is very uncommon. People with allergies may be more sensitive, so be sure to tell your doctor about any allergies you have. An allergy is a sensitivity to certain substances, often pollens or food. Allergies can lead to sneezing, itching, and skin rashes.

Some people have an allergic reaction to immunization injections.

What are some diseases for which immunization is recommended?

- **Diphtheria** can cause a severe sore throat and attack the heart and nervous system.
- **Tetanus** enters the body through an infected wound.
- **Whooping cough** produces violent fits of coughing.
- **Polio** can cause limbs to be permanently weakened.
- **Chickenpox** produces a mild fever and itchy, inflamed blisters or spots.
- **Hepatitis B** causes swelling of the liver, fever, and weakness.
- **Bacterial meningitis** causes swelling of the membranes around the brain and spinal cord.
- **Measles** causes high fevers, cough, and a rash.
- **Mumps** produces fever and swelling of the throat.

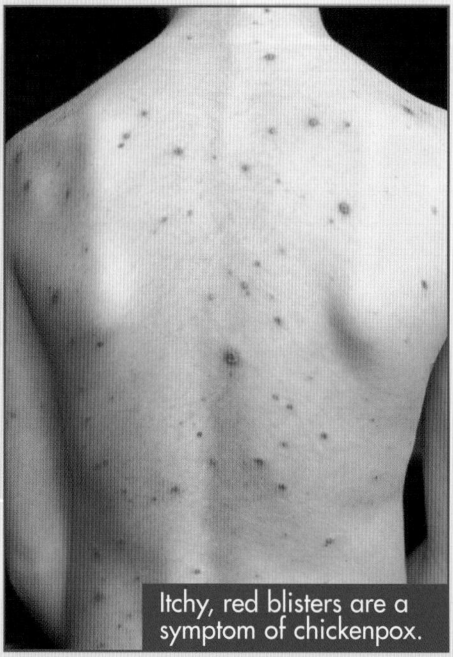
Itchy, red blisters are a symptom of chickenpox.

What is leukemia?

Leukemia is a cancer that affects the cells that form blood in bone marrow. In leukemia, white blood cells that are immature start to multiply very quickly. The white blood cells also interfere with the making of other blood parts, such as platelets. Leukemia used to be one of the most difficult cancers to treat. But today, new methods of treatment have helped to increase the survival rate of people with the disease.

How is leukemia diagnosed?

The doctor will order a blood test. If the blood test shows too many white blood cells, this may suggest leukemia. The doctor will then do a biopsy. A biopsy is a test in which a small amount of bone marrow is removed. The samples will be checked to see if there are any cancer cells.

Symptoms of Leukemia

- tiredness
- paleness
- repeated infections
- weight loss
- bleeding from gums and nose
- bruising

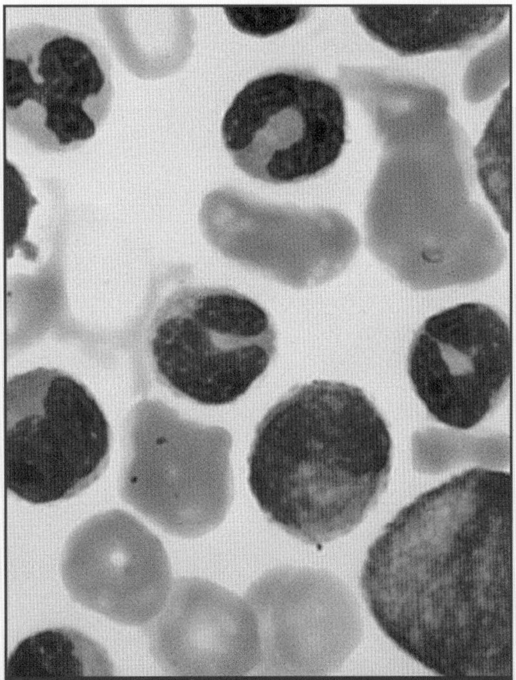

Cancer cells in bone marrow

How is leukemia treated?

Chemotherapy

In chemotherapy, special drugs are used to kill the cancer cells. Chemotherapy has side effects on some normal body cells, such as the cells in the digestive tract, the hair, and bone marrow.

Side effects may cause people who have chemotherapy to feel sick and vomit. They may lose their hair and have more infections. A break between treatments gives the normal cells time to recover.

Bone Marrow Transplant

Doctors can transplant bone marrow from a healthy person to a sick person. First they kill off all the sick bone marrow using chemicals or radiation. Then they inject the healthy bone marrow into the blood. The blood carries the bone marrow cells to the bones. If all goes well, these healthy cells can start to make new blood cells in about three weeks.

Chemotherapy can cause hair loss.

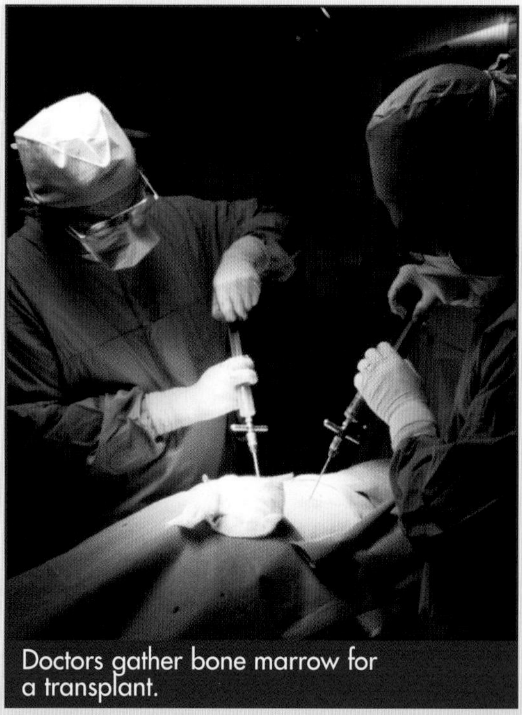

Doctors gather bone marrow for a transplant.

Apply the Key Concepts

Key Concept 1 All organisms are made up of cells that carry out processes that are needed to live.

Activity

Think about all of the things that blood cells do. Draw a concept web showing the processes that these cells carry out in the body.

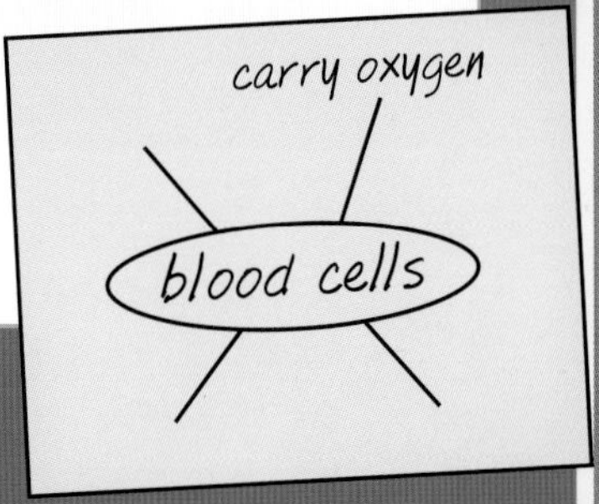

Key Concept 2 Specialized cells perform specialized functions in organisms.

Activity

Create a fact sheet about blood cells. Choose three specialized functions of blood cells. Then, in your own words, write a few sentences for each one explaining why this function is important in keeping the body healthy.

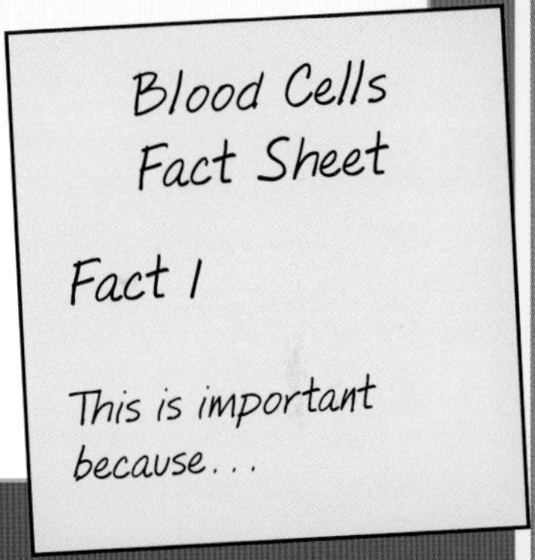

Key Concept 3 Sometimes cells get a disease or become damaged and don't function as they should.

Activity

Create a two-column chart that explains how disease or damage affects blood cells. Label the first column "Disease or Damage" and the second column "Effects."

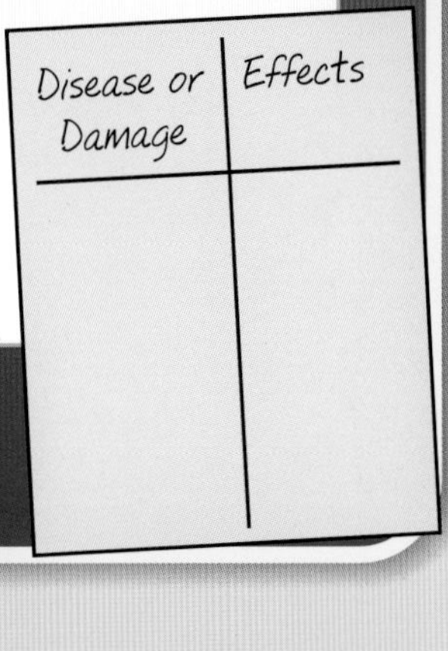

RESEARCH AND WRITE

Create Your Own Pamphlet

An informational pamphlet is a short booklet that gives people information about a topic or issue.

1. Study the Model

Look back at the description of an informational pamphlet on page 18. Then read the informational pamphlet on pages 19–26 again. Notice how the pamphlet is organized. Can you see how the headings help organize the information? Can you find the lists? What details did the writer include to make the text informative? In what ways did these details add interest to the topic?

Writing an Informational Pamphlet

- Keep the information brief and include important facts.
- Use headings to organize the information. Questions often make good headings.
- Use pictures to add interest.
- Include checklists.

2. Choose Your Topic

Get together with others to choose a general topic. Divide the topic up. For example, the topic of *Staying Healthy* can be divided up into smaller topics such as *Healthy Eating* and *Healthy Exercise*. Have each person choose a part of the topic he or she is interested in. You are now ready to research and write an informational pamphlet.

3. Research Your Topic

Ask yourself what you already know about this topic. Do you know enough to write an informational pamphlet? Probably not. So you need to make a list of questions that you will want to answer in your pamphlet. Remember that you need to focus on useful information. Think about what your reader might like or need to know. Now go to the library or to the Internet to get answers to your questions.

My Topic: Recycling

1. What is it?
2. Who should do it?
3. How does it work?
4.

4. Take Notes

Take notes of what you learn. As you gather new information, you may find that it leads to another question. Write the new questions down so that you don't forget them.

5. Write a Draft

Look back at the facts you found. Do they answer the questions you started with, or do you need to include new questions? Start writing your draft, putting your questions and answers in an order that makes sense. If you need to, review the features of an informational pamphlet on page 18.

6. Revise and Edit

Reread your draft. Have you kept the information brief and to the point? Have you included any information that you could present as a checklist?

SHARING YOUR WORK

Create a Display of Pamphlets

Follow the steps below to turn your draft into a pamphlet. Then you can share your work with your classmates.

Make and Share Your Pamphlet

1. Arrange the text.
Fold a piece of paper in half for a four-page pamphlet. Put the title information on the front page. Arrange the rest of the text on the pages. At the top of each page there should be a question followed by information that answers the question. Use the pamphlet in your book as a guide.

2. Include visuals.
Include visuals on your pamphlet to help clarify the information. Be sure your visuals have captions and labels.

3. Create a display.
Post everyone's pamphlets on a bulletin board or lay them out on a table where others can read them.

4. Share and read.
Choose a pamphlet other than the one you wrote. Read it to learn more about its topic. Remember to look for the big ideas as you read.

Glossary

bone marrow – spongy material in the center of bones where blood cells are made

cell membrane – outer covering of the cell

cells – the smallest living parts of organisms

clot – to form into a mass and become solid

cytoplasm – the jelly-like substance that fills a cell, not including the nucleus

disease – a condition that keeps an organism from working as it should

hemoglobin – a red substance in blood cells that carries oxygen around the body

nucleus – the central part of a cell that controls what the cell does

nutrients – substances in food that are needed for life and growth

organisms – all living things, including animals, plants, and single-celled life-forms

plasma – the liquid part of blood

platelets – tiny cell-like disks that help in the process of clotting blood

specialized – able to perform one special task or function

structure – the way all the parts of something fit together

Index